To

Earline

Stand

Keep the faith
it will out for you

3/21/04

Stand

SHARON A. FLOYD

ISBN: 0-8187-0315-6

Edited by Writer's Aide Service, Southfield, MI

Printed by Harlo Printing, Detroit, MI

Table of Contents

Dedication

I dedicate this book to Lilla Darby, my dear departed mother, Artie E. Darby, Sr., father; Lester Floyd, husband and friend; and Christina Floyd and Angelice Renee Floyd, daughters.

I also dedicate this book to my dearest friends who have consulted and supported me during the most difficult times of my career: Clarence E. Berger, Sr., Pastor; Christine Berger, late Co-pastor; Richard Thomas, mentor; and Carol Zak, friend and mentor.

This book is based on my real life experiences in the corporate world.

I was employed by a company in Detroit, Michigan, for 23 years, where I was beset by an internal network of harassers. I will not disclose the name of the company nor will I disclose the identify of the harassers. All names mentioned in this book are fictitious.

During this period, I found a wonderful companion, had two beautiful children, gained sincere friends and achieved a college degree. For 19 and a half years, I enjoyed a good job with excellent benefits and successfully obtained almost every position that I applied for. There was a corporate ladder, and I was climbing it very fast.

Then someone wanted me to compromise my morals, but my strong convictions would not allow me to turn from God's statutes for higher status. I was enthusiastic, conscientious, faithful, hard working and a team player; I thought I could not be harmed, but I found myself enduring harassment and discrimination. "The network" tried to take my ladder and destroy my character, but I persevered. I am still climbing by God's grace.

I have asked, "why me?" There was no reason for me to receive this treatment; neither did I have any control over the string of terrible events that occurred. Surely, God intended me to go through this mishap to prove that He is more powerful and gives hope to others; it was one of my purposes in life.

My methods to overcome harassment differed, depending on the moment of my trials. I was made

Introduction

strong through the Holy Scriptures, loved ones, friends, preaching, and other resources. Standing against the powerful and the popular, I prevailed as David did standing against Goliath. Each time the antidote was different. When all efforts of resolution in the company failed, I received supernatural strength and determination from my faith, believing that if I continued to seek help eventually I would find it. Although I was outnumbered and weak, righteousness prevailed.

Divinely inspired, I write for you and other workers. This book is meant to be practical, as well as inspirational, addressing the steps you must take to resolve your problems in the work place. It is intended to nurture your mind, body and soul, teaching you how to overcome harassment in the work place. It will show you how to get management on your side and teach you how to recover from traumatic experiences at work. You will learn what personal attributes are necessary and what to do and where to go when company mechanisms do not resolve your problems.

As a born-again minister of the gospel of Jesus Christ, I write to strengthen the afflicted, regardless of race, religion or color. As a ready writer, I write to visionaries and achievers who are striving for success and self-fulfillment. As one on a mission, I dare to share the most difficult pressures and unusual experiences to make a statement: You can overcome harassment, achieve your aspirations and joyfully continue to live to the fullest. You can also learn to forgive, as I did.

Though it was extremely painful, I was called to this mission to learn to boldly stand against unrighteousness and to help others out of their desperate places. Too many people are in despair, having lost hope in their dreams because of harassment in the workplace. I learned that forgiveness is a component of love, which is the first fruit of God's spirit. I learned that forgiveness is life and hate is self-destructive. I had to choose between the two, between life and death of the spirit, and I chose correctly; I chose life.

The work force includes people who can make you laugh or make you cry. There are people who can make you lose sleep and destroy your mental and physical well-being. I have even encountered people who practice mind-control and witchcraft to manipulate and control others. Surprisingly, they maintain high paying positions in corporations. Through all my experiences, I have treasured my good relationships and withstood harassment. My dearest friends and acquaintances work at this company and continue to be my major supporters; I will cherish their friendship for the rest of my life.

Reflect on your own life as you read about mine.

It is easy to ignore wrongdoing in hopes that it will eventually go away. Then I learned that evil was like a cancer that had to be diagnosed and treated in its earliest stages or it becomes fatal. Our problems are the same way – whether at work or at home – they too must be identified and addressed before anything positive can take place.

I believe that God gives talents and abilities to everyone at conception. Therefore, all people are of worth and have something valuable to contribute to society. Many times we overlook our talents and abilities that could make us great. As humans, we emulate others

Introduction

and hope to become like them because we have not discovered the good that exists within. Therefore, I challenge you to search your soul; know who you are and what talents you possess. Take note of your strengths and weaknesses and identify any habits that could contribute to problems in the workplace.

1: The Foundation

Whosoever cometh to me and heareth my sayings and doeth them, I will show you to whom he is like: He is like a man which built an house and digged deep and laid the foundation on a rock, and when the flood arose, the stream beat vehemently upon that house and could not shake it; for it was founded upon a rock.

St. Luke 6:47-48

My character and ideas of survival were developed at home, at church and amongst friends. As a child, I was taught to work and overcome obstacles. As a Christian, I was taught that I am more than a conqueror in Christ Jesus. Parental guidance and spiritual teachings were the tools that helped me survive extreme pressures in the work place. Every trial prepared me for life's challenges that were yet to come, and through it all I never lost hope for tomorrow.

I was the oldest of three children born to Artie Darby, Sr. and Lilla M. Darby in Detroit on July 18, 1956. My father came from Jonesville, South Carolina, to obtain the American dream. My mother came from Connellsville, Pennsylvania, to share it. I lived in comfortable but humble surroundings, in neighborhoods consisting of lower-income, African-American people who were proud of their existence. Support and love filled the schools, community and neighborhoods.

Both my parents worked when they were children. My mother picked blackberries and sold lemonade on a dusty country road, and my father cropped the fields in the heat of the day. They learned the value of work at an early age. Even today, my father is a very tall large man who exhibits almost supernatural physical strength. Although he obtained only a 10th grade education, he

1: The Foundation

mastered many trades and possessed excellent problem solving skills.

In 1954, a major company hired him as an electrician, and he met all challenges with his fearless nature and determination to survive. As a rigger responsible for moving large pieces of equipment such as transformers, generators and motors, he was warned that several engineers planned to discredit him when he followed through on a job assignment to move a generator in a plant. My father thanked the tipster who warned him that he was being set up but continued with his job because he knew he was the best rigger in his field. He reported to the engineering group where he was given a blueprint and instructions, which consisted of advanced mathematical calculations and engineering equations. Apparently someone knew about his limited education and thought that the blueprint would frustrate him or even intimidate him. Calmly, he asked the engineers to show him the site where the equipment was to be installed. Once the engineer directed him to the site, my father analyzed the space and the size of the equipment. Then with precision, he compared his job knowledge to the blueprint and determined that the print was incorrect. He reported that there was no possible way to install the equipment according to the specifications given. The engineers marveled at his ability to correct their error despite his inability to understand the formulas. He did not have advanced algebra, nor did he seek help from those who possessed higher education; instead he used his "common sense" to resolve the problem. There was no fear — just another challenge conquered.

1: The Foundation

Mother was a beautician and did millinery work. For 20 years, she worked endlessly in the beauty shop until the fumes from pressed hair overwhelmed her lungs. My sister, brother and I spent many days and nights in the beauty shop. Even with her condition, she continued to work at home to help pay bills. Later on, she became a teacher's aide at Jamieson Elementary School. She obtained her Associates degree in Liberal Arts at a local community college while raising her grandchildren. Many religious leaders and professionals visited her for advice.

Her love, inspiration, wisdom, spiritual insight and physical strength were phenomenal. Her motto was that "one must never give up," and she always gave me encouragement – even in the smallest things. I remember when I was about 7 years old, we'd walked about three miles to Sunday School and stayed for services. After church we came home for dinner and then walked back to church in the late afternoon, returning home again while the evening was still young. I was full of energy and ran most of the way, turning every so often to see mother a few blocks behind. Although she was tired and far behind, she'd encourage me by yelling "S h a r o n keep going."

Although she is silenced in her grave, her voice of encouragement rings in my soul. It was her way of saying that she may not obtain the promise, but her children must continue to strive to attain the prize. The vivid picture of her calling to me to keep going never leaves me, and I see life as a relay race with one generation achieving what it can before the next generation picks up the banner and continues toward the goal.

2: Destiny versus Decision

Trust in the Lord with all thine heart, and lean not unto thine own understanding. In all thy ways acknowledge him, and he shall direct thy paths.

Proverbs 3:5-6

Both my parents stressed work ethics: maintaining good attendance, performing excellent work and working well with others. These principles continue to be my paradigm regardless of the discrimination and harassment that I have encountered in recent years.

After attending Jamieson Elementary School, I went to McMichael Jr. High School, a neighborhood school, where I developed an interest in helping others. I started volunteering my time to tutor children, and on Saturdays I looked forward to working with children who needed assistance with their academics, whatever the subject.

I graduated from McMichael Jr. High School and attended Northwestern High School, where I continued to tutor. One day, during my senior year in high school, my counselor called me to her office. As I walked down the hallways, I thought about other students who received office calls and tried to guess what had happened to my mother, sister or brother? Was I not going to graduate this year? What had I done wrong? Anxiety gripped me, and my steps became shorter and slower until I reached the office.

When I reached the office, the counselor invited me to have a seat. She said that the Detroit Public School System had been following the progress of my students over the years. Apparently, all had improved greatly and

2: Destiny versus Decision

maintained good grades. Therefore, the Detroit Public School System wanted to reward me with a college scholarship, all expenses paid, to attend Wayne State University and obtain a degree in education. Upon receiving my teaching degree, I was to return to the neighborhood to teach at Jamieson Elementary School. Although I was flattered, my ultimate dream was to become a successful manager in the corporate world. I told my counselor that I was grateful but that "teachers did not make enough money." I had plans to get a degree in business administration and become a manager in a corporation. I was unsure how I was going to get a degree in business administration because I did not have any money for college, but I had a dream that seemed reachable and faith to make it possible.

Periodically, since the harassment began, I wonder if I made the right career decision. My aspirations meant more to me than an opportunity at hand. It's human nature to overlook our natural talents in hopes of becoming like someone else. But our natural talents are drivers that allow us to fulfill our purpose in life. I believe that a special ability is deposited during conception – an ability that appears to be so natural it predestines one for success. According to my family tree, I come from a lineage of educators and counselors. Ironically, I am now tutoring at-risk children, ages 2-4, as a volunteer through the Parent-Child Home Development Program of Detroit.

To achieve my business goals, I attended business school for two years and got an entry-level job as a clerk typist in a corporation, followed in short order by a position as senior typist and then one as stenographer. When, I got my Associates degree in Business Administration, I immediately obtained a semi–professional position as a business technician. These quick successes gave me the incentive to continue my education. I was a fast tracker, and there was no stopping me.

After three years of employment, I married Lester Floyd, an electrical engineer, whom I met at the company where I worked. Two years later we had a daughter, Christina. Although I was wearing many hats, I did not stop educating myself; most of my evenings were spent in night school. Somehow I even found time to evangelize during the week and attend Sunday services.

*But now thus saith the Lord that created thee, O Jacob, and he
that formed thee, O Israel. Fear not: For I have redeemed thee.
I have called thee by thy name; thou art mine. When thou
passeth through the waters, I will be with thee, and through
the rivers, they shall not overflow thee. When thou walketh
through the fire, thou shalt not be burned, neither shall the
flame kindle upon you.*

Isaiah 43: 1-3

My mother, who was a minister, traveled with me to
women's retreats and to revivals. She was my confidant,
friend and prayer partner; my mother believed in me.
She encouraged me to continue my higher education and
hoped to see me graduate from college. Although I
noticed that her eyes had become dim, her hair had
thinned and her steps were slow, I was too busy in
college to see what was coming until, in 1989, I received
a call at work. My mother was scheduled to go into
surgery for breast removal because of cancer, and the
people at the hospital were asking me to be present
during the surgery. I was devastated by the news because my mother had not told any of my family that she
was ill.

I told my boss about the situation and left work
immediately, praying for a successful outcome. While
driving to the hospital, I thought about my aunt (my
mother's youngest sister) who had died from breast
cancer about 10 years before and how my mother had
always talked about my aunt's suffering. During the
entire surgery, which lasted three hours, I sat at a small
round table in the waiting room and prayed fervently.

I saw my mother in the intensive care unit (ICU)
right after surgery. Although, she was bright, beautiful

3: The Hardest Trial

and in high spirits, the events of the day seemed overwhelming. I could not be equally bright and cheerful. As I walked towards her, I teetered on my feet, and the nurses ran to catch me, insisting that I sit down and drink orange juice to regain my strength. When the doctor came in to give his report, he found me still sitting. He told me the surgery was successful, but the cancer had already spread to the bones.

My mother, confident that God was in control of her destiny, handled the bad news with grace and courage. Later, I learned that the cancer had been developing for eight years, during which time she did not seek any medical treatment. She always managed to put off her personal needs to help others and preach the Gospel of Jesus of Christ. At the time, she was raising my sister's two daughters who were 6 and 4 years old. Perhaps God allowed her to live that long with cancer to be an example of victorious Christian living in the midst of sufferings. "For if we suffer with him, we will reign with him."

As I sat next to my mother in the recovery room, I sensed that she would not be with me for long. Somehow, I felt that I had to fulfil as many of her dreams as soon as possible. Questions began to race in my mind. What could possibly comfort her? What memories could be made for her to cherish? What promises could be fulfilled before she entered into eternity? Overwhelmed by my thoughts and fears, I prayed that God would give me the answers and that He would give us the strength to handle whatever trials that were ahead. After many days and nights of meditation, I decided to focus on goals that could be accomplished within two years.

3: The Hardest Trial

Over the years, Mother had encouraged me to get a Master's degree, cherishing the moment when she would see me graduate from college. This became my first goal. To achieve it, I had to complete four years of night school in two years. At the same time, I did not want to give up any time with her. I wanted to dine out with her, shop with her, take her to women's retreats and spend quality time with her. Doing everything I wanted to do required a commitment from me as well as total support and understanding from my husband and 7-year-old daughter.

Lester has always been a responsible, caring person who valued family living. He understood what I needed to do, and he supported me by taking over the household chores and providing most of the care for our daughter, Christina. He still jokes about how his friends thought that he was a widower because Christina went to the golf courses with him.

For two years my typical day would be: Wake up and go to work, leave work and race to night class, visit with Mother. Enthusiasm and determination helped me meet the pressures of life. Six months after surgery, Mother's health began to rapidly deteriorate, and the EMS frequently transported her to the hospital. Many times I went to the hospital with my books to study for tests and a bible to comfort and pray with her. Often I did not get home until 2 a.m., waking up just a few hours later to start the hectic routine all over again.

Although I passed all of my tests with high scores, I found it difficult to deal with the simplest matters. To complicate my life further, I was assigned to learn computer programming at work, which added to the stress of my daily routine. So much concentration during the day at work and at night on completing my degree left me fatigued. Once, I blacked out while driving and hit a car in front of me. Fortunately, I was driving at a slow speed so the person in the other car was only slightly injured.

Finally, I was in my last semester. Time was short; Mother could not walk or even sit for any length of time. By the end of the semester, she was in bed for longer and longer periods. I knew that she would not be able to attend my commencement ceremonies. On commencement day, I could not truly celebrate with joy because my great accomplishment was mixed with pain and sorrow.

After graduation, family members took me out to Carl's Chop House, an elegant restaurant, to honor my achievement. I went from there to my mother's house to find the house dark and Mother alone. Mother was dying; her breathing had become weak and sporadic. I put on my cap and clenching my degree in both hands, said, "Mother, I did it. I got my degree!" She opened her eyes and immediately regained enough strength to sit up. Death backed away, as new life flowed into her.

The day after graduation, my manager called me to his office and told me to interview for a professional job as a market researcher. It was the first job that I did not have to apply for; my manager had arranged an interview for me because he was very pleased with my work. My graduation, which occurred just as a reorganization was taking place, allowed me to embark immediately on a professional career in the corporation. My dreams were coming true.

3: The Hardest Trial

The gentleman who conducted the interview was Caucasian, middle aged and stout. He had black wavy hair, accented with silver. He wore a navy blue suit, a white shirt and a subdued blue tie. My first impression was that he was very distinguished, very charming and very much in control. I felt it an honor to be in his presence. As I peered at his eyes during the interview, they seemed to change colors from light blue to icy gray. I sensed that there were hidden depths to this man, but I took a positive view. Confidently, I answered all of his questions and expressed my eagerness to began my professional career in Marketing. It was a perfect beginning, and it is still hard for me to believe that this man would ultimately seek to destroy my character.

Within the week, I learned that I had been accepted for the position in Marketing. My mother rejoiced with me about this accomplishment. That night we shared precious memories, and she talked to me of the days when she played baseball at the Sunday School picnic, making me laugh for hours. I remember her hitting a ball, running to third base on it, and attempting to make it home – sliding in as the pitcher and base man closed in on her. The crowd was silent, waiting breathlessly for the umpire's call. As the dust settled, the umpire could be seen with both hands stretched out. "Safe!" he shouted.

That night was the best going-away gift she could ever give me, but our joy was short lived. Two months later, Mother died.

4: When Trouble Comes

When the enemy shall come in like a flood, the Spirit of the Lord shall lift up a standard against him.

Isaiah 59:19

Because I never had work problems, I did not recognize trouble when it came. I would overlook offenses, wishing them away. As you read this chapter, perhaps you will recognize the signs of trouble in your life and learn to deal effectively with situations as they occur and visualize God's divine intervention working for the good.

I noticed that the employees in Marketing entertained lifestyles that were not in tune with Christian principles and that they were supported in these actions by senior executives. There was drinking after hours and all kinds of goings on with male co-workers. I wondered if good works and intelligence would be sufficient for me to succeed. I was working with people who were very blatant about their personal desires.

Regardless of my personal convictions, I had to learn to work with these people who were very different and express my limits to co-workers without being offensive. My personal goal was to be a worker who made outstanding contributions to the company. I vowed to reach my goals by providing exceptional work and allowing my team members to take the credit for it. It was my way of gaining acceptance in the inner circles.

Trace, the distinguished man who interviewed me, was neither a director nor a supervisor, but he had considerable control over most of the Marketing department and influenced the decisions of interdepartmental activities. Often Trace met with directors and other senior executives to advise and counsel them. I was impressed by his influence, professionalism and power and thought that if I'd prove myself to him he would be my route to future promotions.

I wanted to be accepted in the higher ranks as a professional. Another side of me wanted to be liked by others. In the process of trying to please everyone, I made the mistake of exalting leaders. It was a holdover from the way I was raised. During the early years of my employment, people moved up the ranks by showing their devotion to the company, working long hours and proving themselves on the job. Community work and a stable home life also counted. The leaders in these days led with the rod of iron, the excellence of Daniel and the wisdom of Solomon. Surely they were vessels of honor, and I aspired to be like them.

But good morals and good work on the job are not required of today's leaders. Television and the papers were reporting numerous incidents of corruption and adultery among our nation's leaders, but I was too focused on what was happening in my own life to pay attention to what was happening around me. I just assumed that people in certain positions were good role models, but that assumption was no longer true.

Leadership and good morals were not one and the same thing by the time I started to move up in the corporate world. Young executives were being hired for their ability to adapt quickly to new environments, not for their job experience or loyalty to the company. Attracted by large salaries, they stayed only until someone offered them more money. Their attitude was "self gain without pain," and during hard times they've been the ones most likely to "abandon the ship."

4: When Trouble Comes

The mistake I made was to depend on Trace to make me successful. When I stopped relying on God and looked to Trace and other market executives, I was sowing the seeds of my problems. These people did not possess the deep inner qualities of leadership that I had known and cherished. I did not realize that they handed out promotions only to those who were part of "the network," regardless of job experience.

Every day, I strived to be a valuable employee to the organization. Although I was inexperienced in marketing, Trace Rivers gave me very high profile assignments, which enriched my work experience and corporate exposure. I was thankful and showed it by providing top quality work and getting exceptional results. Trace worked very closely with me, requesting my services for all his major projects and overlooking more experienced researchers. As a result, my fellow workers began to resent me for the opportunities I was given. Working day and night, enjoying every moment of this time, I was too focused on my work to realize what was going on in his mind and in the minds of others.

The mixed signals came through as he communicated about the assignments. At one meeting, he boldly stated, "Sharon is mine, and if you give her any problems you will have to deal with me." The room became very quiet. Some men raised their eyebrows, while others grinned. I wanted to address the comment, but I was quieted by the possible consequences and my feelings of shame. My embarrassment kept me silent for days.

I struggled with what Trace could possibly have meant by the statement and what the other professionals might be thinking. I felt humiliated. Even worse, I felt guilty for his behavior and tried to determine how I could have contributed to his actions. Rather than pulling him aside to address the issue and my concerns, I chose to overlook it and hoped that nothing further would happen.

But the problem intensified and moved to a spiritual level. I remember praying about the job situation one night and praying to God for my needs. The next morning Trace met me at the elevator and repeated my prayer verbatim. I was so startled, my mouth opened as I tried to determine how he knew what I had prayed for during my quiet time in the privacy of my bedroom. I became very uncomfortable with him because it seemed that he knew what I was thinking at all times. Once he even said that he was going to make me think about him day and night. I found that on most days we were even wearing the same colors. I felt entrapped and wondered what I could do to get out of his reach.

I could feel the shadow of his presence at home while I slept, while I was with friends, while I drove in my car, everywhere except while I attended services at church. Only there, where the power of God prevailed, was there no evil, no mind control and no witchcraft. Daily my thoughts were totally consumed with him. Many times as I sat at my desk, I would feel his overwhelming presence trying to possess me. As I struggled with several emotions, I sat paralyzed. My eyes welled up, and big warm tears streamed uncontrollably down my face. I was in a deep inner battle that tormented me and left me mentally exhausted and spiritually hungry. How could I break this unhealthy connection that was leaving me spiritually battered.

I prayed to God, and a still, small voice said. "Speak in tongues (Acts 1:8; 2:1-4), and he will become confused; he won't be able to connect with you, nor will he be able to understand your prayers."

I began to pray in tongues, and the following day Trace's confidence was totally shattered. I observed him running in and out of his office, keeping his distance from me. This was the first sign that he was not in total control. Finally, the invisible tie – the spiritual connection was broken.

I worked diligently for Trace over a two-year period, and he received two promotions in that time. Never once did he speak on my behalf. I thought he would use his influence to promote me as well, but he didn't. Nevertheless, I congratulated him on each promotion and showed my support. I was reluctant to let go of my hope that he would recognize how much I contributed to his projects.

It took me a while to realize that Trace never wanted to use his influence on my behalf. In fact, he was working against me.

One day he asked me to forgive him because he had told lies about me. Several directors had asked Trace about my credentials, and he had told them negative things to keep me on his team. Then he told me, "You are mine. You belong to me, and I cannot let my good thing go." I was speechless then. I didn't say anything to him for shame and my feelings of indebtedness to him. After all, he gave me assignments that provided me with experience and exposure. But I did not tell anyone about his behavior. For almost 20 years, I had maintained a good work record, never complaining or making waves.

4: When Trouble Comes

Now that I had something to complain about, I did not know where to start. I didn't even want to start; I didn't want to bring any negative attention to myself.

Quietly, I retreated by making myself unavailable to him. If I was not an eager team player, perhaps he would not longer use me for his self gain. Then I could consider my debt to him as paid. I began to take projects from other marketing executives. After I ignored him for two weeks, Trace called me to his desk to ask why I hadn't offered my services to him. I told him that I had been very busy with other assignments. He advised me not to work for the others because "I was not their slave," meaning that I was "his slave." It amazed me to discover that the ancient mind set of a "master-slave mentality" still exists. It's the same attitude my great, great grandparents, my great grandparents, my grandparents and, to some extent, my parents had to overcome. Now it was my turn to overcome.

There is a spiritual logic to this. Evil, hatred and oppression are spiritual entities that don't die. They live from generation to generation in our bodies, thoughts and behaviors – until a spiritual conversion takes place. Even after the conversion, these evil spirits fight to regain their place in our minds and hearts. Regardless of my contributions, this man was showing no respect for me as a human being and a professional, even though he had benefited tremendously from my efforts.

I continued my work for others. When Trace saw that I ignored his advice, he called me to his desk. His eyes were a bone-chilling gray. With determination in his voice, he said, "I am going to destroy you and break your spirit."

I should have challenged him about his using the word "slave." I should have countered his words of destruction with the Word of God. I should have reported the conversations to our bosses. I should have had courage, but I chose to remain quiet. As I pondered his statements, I couldn't believe he meant what he said, and my disbelief gave me false hope. How could he be so blatant?

I walked away thinking about how I had faithfully and diligently contributed to his success and how I was being repaid. A feeling of deep anguish filled my soul. I found myself almost compietely disheartened. There is always a moment when the burden seems unbearable, but even at such moments we are not alone. There was peace and prayer, encounters of the closest kind with friends or family. There were gestures of love given to me in special ways; there were Scriptures to encourage me, and always there were the strong arms of God to deliver me from all of my enemies.

God is our refuge and strength, a very present help in the time of trouble.

Psalms 46:1

I learned that God does not waste his time with the preliminaries. We expect God to deliver us before we have a true encounter because we do not want to feel pain. But only when trouble arrives does God address it and in a blink of an eye eliminate it. As quickly as trouble came, God appeared and gave me victory so that I would not suffer shame.

I thought that I had seen and heard it all, when something unusual happened. I normally ate lunch in

4: When Trouble Comes

the cafeteria with friends, but one day I had a strong urge to be alone. It was a beautiful summer day and I took my lunch to the patio where I met two friends. We enjoyed a good conversation while eating our lunch, but after a while I longed to be even more solitary. I felt drawn to excuse myself. I slowly walked through the corridors, hoping to take a short nap before my lunch break ended. I sat down at my desk, laid my head down and closed my eyes. After a few minutes, Trace came to my office, but he did not see me. I was awake but remained motionless to see his intentions. Trace went directly to my book case and picked up my name tag; then he used his three fingers to trace my name. When he stopped, he turned the tag upside down and placed it back on the book shelf. He was so deeply involved in his ritual that he did not notice me. While he was walking away, I called to him, startling him. He immediately said that he was looking for my supervisor and hurried away.

At that point, I suspected that Trace was involved in witchcraft or mysticism. Although I was not knowledgeable about the subject, I felt that he was performing a ritual to send an evil spell on me. This was harassment of a different kind. I saw real evil, destruction and deception at work. I knew that I was not fighting against flesh and blood but against spiritual wickedness in high places. Trace was a ruler in the enemy's army, and he seemed unstoppable. Yet, I believed that God had His agenda as well, which was to tear down this kingdom of evil in the work place. I was the tool selected for this purpose. Instinctively, I knew how to deal with the problem. I knew I could win battles and even some wars with the help of the Creator.

Walking past Trace's office, I noticed a book that bore an occult symbol. Compelled to see what Trace was reading, I quickly picked it up. More evil was revealed. The book was a true crime story of a serial killer and included detailed descriptions of killings, child sacrifices and other gruesome acts of violence. After reading the back of the book and a few pages inside, chills ran down my spine. How could such an intelligent person take pleasure in reading about serial killings and human sacrifices? Then I realized that there was no limit to what this person would do to gain power and control.

To keep my spirits lifted, I went to a women's retreat and brought many tapes for meditation. When I returned to work, several Christians who also attended the conference visited me to speak of what we had heard. Trace overheard some of these discussions and took the opportunity, when I was alone, to ask me about the conference. I was elated because this was my chance to witness to him about Jesus. The thought of helping convert him brought joy to my soul. I thought that by sharing one of the tapes from the conference with him, I would be an instrument to turn his life around. He took the tape home with him and commented to me the next day that everything he heard on the cassette was true. Then he quickly suggested that I read something dear to him. It was a book on "the power of the mind and mind control." I was shocked and disappointed at his assumption that I would be interested in such subjects. Taking a stand for my beliefs, I declined to read the book, stating that Christians don't practice mind control.

In that moment, many of the questions I had about the invisible tie in our business relationship were answered. I was close to the source of "the network," but

4: When Trouble Comes

Trace realized what had happened. He saw me as a hindrance and became more deliberate in his efforts to destroy me. He had worked closely enough with me to know my strengths and weaknesses. He knew that I took pride in my work and focused on it to the point of being nearsighted. He used these qualities against me, by giving me assignments that were not humanly possible to complete, knowing I would not give up on them.

Once, for example, he insisted that I gather statistics from the Census Bureau and the company's Computer Information System and manually compute the numbers. When I started on this assignment, a computer programmer came by and asked me what I was doing. After giving him the details of the project, he informed me that only a computer could do such an assignment. He then developed a macro program that gathered and calculated the data. It took that program 90 computer hours to complete the statistical calculations that I was told to perform manually. Instead of being destroyed, I was victorious. God sent a computer specialist to write the program that met my needs. I had time to relax. When trouble comes, God's standard supersedes the plans of the enemy. I took the yoke of Jesus who said, "take my yoke upon you and learn of me, for my yoke is easy and my burden is light."

But winning one battle did not mean I had won the war. There were frequent skirmishes, and anguish infiltrated my mind. Over a period of time, I became so stressed I lost hair in spots. In my body, fibroid tumors grew from the size of quarters to the size of grapefruits in a three-month period. I had to have them surgically removed.

4: When Trouble Comes

Trace had deep feelings for me, ranging from love to hate, and he seemed capable of sustaining both simultaneously. He sought opportunities to make amends, right after causing me grief. After my operation, he made a special effort to send me exotic flowers, the most beautiful I had ever seen. When I returned to work, he began to touch me more often. He'd caress my cheeks and stroke my shoulders. Tears of torment ran down my face as his advances grew more intense.

I prayed for wisdom and God answered, "blame yourself for his shortcomings and tell him that your upbringing doesn't allow you to be caressed."

I had the answer but I needed courage. The next morning, I went to him and said that I would like to talk to him about something that had been bothering me. The conversation went something like this: "The other day you brought pictures of your dog and your home, showing your warmth and friendliness. I know that you are a warm person and don't mean to upset me when you caress my cheeks, stroke my flesh or ask me out after work, but I do not come from the same background as you. I was taught not to caress or stroke a man unless I planned to have sex with him. That is a sexual stimulus to me, and only my husband is allowed to do it."

He said, "I am glad that you told me because I didn't think I was doing anything wrong. I will be careful not to do it again."

A weight fell from my shoulders. I did not have to worry about his rage or fear his retaliation because of the wisdom I had used in selecting my words. Later, that

4: When Trouble Comes

day he put on his coat and stood silently at the entrance to my office for a period of time. I turned to see him facing me, staring while he buttoned his coat. Then he tightened his belt and left for the day.

Shortly after, Trace gave me an assignment that required extensive research with another company. I was instructed to set up a meeting with two individuals from that company. I was apprehensive about the assignment based on past experience, but I followed instructions. Signing in at the other company just before the meeting, I found Trace inspecting me. Then he said, "I want you to turn on your charm." Stunned by the remark, I wondered what charm had to do with the assignment, but didn't question what he said. The two men met us, and we followed them to an office where the meeting went smoothly. When we left, Trace again made a strange remark, telling me to do what it takes to get what I want. Confused, I stood in the middle of the corridor and pondered his statement. Was I expected to return to the room to be with the other men? Was he expecting me to be a corporate prostitute? I remained silent and got on the elevator with Trace. Twenty minutes after we returned to our company, the assignment was cancelled. When Trace saw that I refused to be used, he gave all my assignments to a co-worker.

When the wicked, even my enemies and my foes came upon me to eat up my flesh, they stumbled and fell. Though a host encamp against me, my heart shall not fear. Though war should rise against me, in this will I be confident.

Psalms 27:2-3

Trace was transferred to another area and four other members of "the network" stepped in to take his place. Like the ruthless man he was, Trace sought to destroy me through "the network," a group of men and women who vowed to work together against me until I'd crack from the stress or become frustrated enough to quit my job of 20 years. Clara, Spikey, James and Fredmond worked collectively and separately against me to achieve their goals. Each player committed a different act of harassment, but all of their actions were related.

The problems really began when Clara was promoted to be my boss. In the organization where I work, promotions are handed out to those who are a part of "the network" regardless of their job experience. Clara had no supervisor's experience, but she was well groomed, very polished and very aggressive. She gave confusing instructions, withheld pertinent information to hinder the progress of the assignments, and discredited and demeaned me before my fellow co-workers and professionals. I knew the reason for her behavior. When she was promoted, two people pulled me aside to warn me that I was targeted to quit the company, either of my own will or forced out.

Trace had manipulated me through flattery; Clara manipulated me through criticism. Both were masters of mind control. Outwardly cordial, Clara did everything she could to deceive and destroy my credibility. The

5: Undermining Credibility

young woman would come to work with a warm smile and a pleasant "good morning," but would make every effort to kill my self-confidence and character. Constantly, she told me that I could not communicate, even though I worked in communications and communicated regularly to the masses. Constantly, she corrected my writing, including notes and memos, adding nothing to the message but attempting to create in me a feeling of inadequacy. One of her more subtle weapons was to give me only half the information required to complete a job. Then she waited until I had almost completed the project to give me the rest of the instructions. Her actions served to reinforce the impression that I was incompetent.

The situation reminded me of a study conducted by Jane Elliott, and described in her documentary "Brown Eyes, Blue Eyes," which showed how discrimination creates incompetence through self-vilification. Ms. Elliott divided a class of children into brown eyes and blue eyes. The first day she made the brown-eyed children wear big collars and told them they were not allowed to drink from the fountains without a cup. They could not play with the blue-eyed children or answer any questions before the blue-eyed children did. They were also told that they were not as smart as the blue-eyed children. After a day of this drilling, the children were tested. The scores of the brown-eyed children were low; even the higher achievers in the group did not do well. But the blue-eyed children excelled. The following day, collars were given to the blue-eyed children and the drilling was reversed. Now the brown-eyed children could do as they pleased. Testing showed that the blue-eyed children were now suffering.

5: Undermining Credibility

It was February 1993 when Clara assigned me to write an article about a government project for the company newsletter. Because Clara generally rewrote my work to break my self-esteem and destroy my self-confidence, the assignment made me very suspicious.

On this day, I was determined to end the humiliation so I contacted a dear friend and fellow Christian who was a director for counsel. She agreed to ask the newsletter editor to look over the article before I submitted it to Clara. Although I was given two weeks to complete the assignment, I worked frantically while on vacation to get a draft to the editor within a week. Surprisingly, the editor asked only two questions and incorporated very minor changes into my draft. After making her changes, I gave a clean draft to the editor and another to Clara. Then Clara met with a friend and proceeded to rewrite the article. She returned it with comments in red on every sentence. I told her that the editor had already reviewed and approved the article. If she had any changes, she would have to take them to the head editor. Clara did so, and there was a big blowout between herself and the editor. Later the editor told me that the changes did not add anything to the context and therefore were unnecessary. Despite what the editor said, the article never made it into print. Although my boss admitted that the changes proposed weren't important, she claimed that my article included competitive information that should not be shared with the public. This justified her demand to stop the printing of the article. One result of the episode was that she stopped editing my work.

5: Undermining Credibility

While Clara accused me of being unable to communicate, her three-year-old son developed severe language problems – to the point where he needed a speech therapist for assistance. I believe that the words she sent to me boomeranged and landed on a weaker vessel, which was her son. I wondered if she ever realized that her own words judged her dearest innocent son. Evil workers often do not realize that their actions harm their loved ones.

I had won this battle, but the war continued. I was constantly battling and my enemies seemed to have supernatural strength. They were tireless, calculating, bold and focused. But I had God on my side.

When Clara gave me a very bad appraisal, I reported her actions to the human resource consultant and to my director, both very close friends with Clara. The consultant went through the motions of listening to me, but nothing was done on my behalf. I was surrounded by members of "the network" who had key positions in the company.

It seemed like I was all alone. Then, in a solemn moment, I looked to the hills from whence comes my help. Revelation from God began to flow from heaven. A vision of a boxer appeared to me. He was extremely masculine, in excellent physical condition and quick on his feet. When his opponent landed punches on his stomach and head, this boxer gave at least three for every one that landed. I determined that he was so fierce in the ring because he was conditioned to take the punches. I began to remember all the times when I needed God the most and He came through.

He was there for my oldest daughter, Christina, who was born with an obstruction of the bile ducts, a potentially fatal liver disease because the bile accumulates in the body and backs up, drowning the person. The doctors did everything they could, but it wasn't enough. My husband immediately lost hope. But my mother, my pastor and his wife came to the hospital and anointed Christina as she lay almost lifeless. We held hands and prayed for a miracle in the name of Jesus. The next day, Christina's liver began to function and the bile ducts opened; a greenish brown fluid flushed out of her body.

I also remembered how God brought me through my mother's death. I realized that my faith and the name of Jesus had conditioned me to take the punches.

For almost 20 years, I had developed excellent work relations throughout the Company and received good appraisals. This would have been my first bad report. I knew I had to counter it immediately; otherwise, future supervisers might believe it to be true.

I went to the vice president and presented the letters of appreciation I had received from several directors, copies of former appraisals, lists achievements and reports that added value to the company. How could I get a director's recommendation in January and a bad evaluation in March from Clara? There were no logical answers. After meeting with the vice president, the appraisal was removed from my corporate file.

6: Defensive Positioning

Ye are all the children of light, and the children of the day. We are not of the night, nor of darkness. Therefore let us not sleep as do others, but let us watch and be sober.

I Thessalonians 4:5-6

The situation worsened when Janet Fuller became my director. Janet was best friends with Clara and no friend of mine, as I discovered when I worked for her during a transition period.

I facilitated a continuous improvement team created to improve customer service and resolve the communication problems that occur during emergencies. Experienced customer representatives shared a wealth of knowledge and exhibited a high level of competence in problem solving. Team meetings were inspirational because openness, honesty and trust were encouraged among team members. We reached many goals within a short period, and I developed a great appreciation for customer representatives as professional communicators.

After three months, a corporate initiative continuous improvement task force was established to resolve problems similar to ours. Some of the facilitators and team members were either in "the network" or new hires who were on the fast track in the company. These lead assignments were intended to give them exposure and justify their future leadership positions.

One of the corporate facilitators was Carl Lowan, an acquaintance of Janet's. Although he was not a producer, he was sheltered by "the network" and popular among others in the leadership circle. Janet told him of my team's progress and encouraged him to capitalize on our efforts. As a result, he boldly insisted that I submit my

6: Defensive Positioning

team's report to him to be incorporated in his final report to the Vice President. I was certain our findings would work to his benefit only and that our team would not get any credit or recognition for our efforts.

I recalled another instance when I did what was asked and then was bypassed when rewards were handed out. At that time, the company was putting together a marketing project for a trade fair that would showcase a new product for customers. Marketing representatives had not solicited many customers and four days before the event only a handful had committed to attend. Then I was assigned to market the project by telephone, along with a project leader and three others. In effect, we were being told to sell a project that had already been written off as a failure.

The project leader was a nervous wreck, and two of the three workers bowed out of what seemed to be a dismal situation. Thank God the third was a born-again Christian and determined to prevail. After reviewing the lists, I received a surge of supernatural faith and energy. I thought about targeting wealthy customers who were most likely to purchase the product. As I began to solicit, words of power, sensitivity and excitement flowed from me like a melody. Describing the coming event in detail, I aroused the curiosity of my listeners. Over a three-day period, working seven hours each day, I made contact with many business owners. Each day, the other Christian and myself prayed to God for a miracle, encouraging each other to victory. Each night, I took my list of customers home, lifted it up to God and prayed further for a miracle. Although the thought of what could occur if the project failed sometimes chilled me, I kept a positive outlook while soliciting customers and realized that by faith something special was about to take place.

On the day of the event, my boss told me that we had to sell 300 items to break even. He was sure we would not reach our goal. The day started slowly, and then about 11:30 a.m., customers began to arrive. A man rustled through the door with pamphlets falling out of his pockets and onto the ground. He seemed to be very disorganized to the point where no one even wanted to register him. I assisted him and learned that he headed a large corporation that needed the product we were selling. Other co-workers who overheard our conversation gathered around me and began to attend to him. He gruffly told them, "if you didn't want to register me when I came in don't break your back to serve me now." As he walked away, I was convinced that we had lost the sale.

The next day, the team leader rushed in to announce success. Apparently the disorganized gentlemen had bought 700 of our product. Another corporation bought 2,000 and a third bought 300. The senior executives wanted to know who had solicited most of the customers, and they learned that I had called most of those who were attending the event by invitation. I received a letter of thanks, but the team leader received the promotion.

I remembered other instances of profits achieved through my efforts and credit going to others. The people who were promoted were the ones who reported the success. They were the liaisons who contributed little but were members of "the network."

6: Defensive Positioning

I vowed this would not happen to me again. When Carl insisted that I share information, threatening me with some vague retribution, I stalled. I informed all of my team members that all inquiries about our team's findings or progress should be referred to me. When Carl's deadline drew near, he became desperate for our report. His demands became more frequent and forceful – the harassment had begun. He told me that the directors were planning to take the continuous improvement effort from me. Later, I learned that he had the support of Janet in this pressure.

I was called into the director's office and given a direct order to submit my team's report to him. I had to make a decision. Should I follow the direct order and lose all, or should I follow my heart? A surge of boldness and courage rose in me. What nerve of them to expect me to give away·all of my team's hard efforts. I decided to take whatever actions necessary to gain recognition and reward for my team and myself.

How could I overcome a conspiracy? I prayed to God for guidance, and the following day I received my answer through a Detroit Pistons basketball game that my daughter was watching. I heard the announcer shout the plays as the teams ran from one side of the court to the other. I heard the cheers when someone made a basket. I heard the crowd shout, "Defense, Defense, Defense."

Defensive positioning is a key play in the corporate world, as well. It involves channeling a dispute to a higher authority when injustice and unfairness are obvious and a heavy hand is required to balance the weights. A clear voice spoke within my soul with firm and sure instructions. "Write a letter to the Vice President, stating the problem, expose the harassment and those who are involved in the conspiracy. Mention similar experiences that you've had in the department. State your argument and offer a resolution to this problem."

That morning I rushed to work early to write my letter. Words began to flow easily as I wrote, following the inspiration of the Holy Spirit. The examples gave a clear picture of the situation, of my contributions that were previously overlooked, of the valuable information that my team had gathered. I recommended that if we were required to submit our package, we should be given appropriate credit and become permanent team members in the corporate initiative. Since I was bringing work to the table, I proposed myself as co-facilitator of the corporate effort. Essentially, I was going after my harasser's leadership position.

The Vice President summoned my director and manager. Shortly after, I was told that the Vice President had granted my terms for sharing information with the corporate initiative continuous team. I was asked to serve on the corporate initiative task force, along with several of my team members. Our team gave an excellent presentation that earned respect and recognition throughout the company. Furthermore, we were also given bonuses for excellent performance.

Carl submitted an incomplete report that had little value. Needless to say, he suffered shame and humiliation and did not cross my path again. The just weights were balanced.

Can the Ethiopian change his skin, or the leopard his spots?
Then may ye also do good that are accustomed to do evil.

Jeremiah 12:23

We are troubled on every side, yet not distressed; we are
perplexed but not in despair; persecuted, but not forsaken; cast
down, but not destroyed.

II Corinthians 4:8-9

A work place is shaped by the management style and attitude of its leaders. Leaders set the pace; they orchestrate and establish fairness for employees. If the leader shows dislike towards certain individuals, employees follow suit. On the other hand, if a leader states that he will not tolerate any unfair practices, the employees mimic that behavior to earn approval.

I felt myself in a vicious circle. Janet was in control of the department, and I had not experienced any measure of fairness from her. I had hopes that she would change her attitude, but evil doers develop their own belief systems. True conversion can only be indicated by God and willingly accepted by the individual. Until someone experiences an inner change of spirit and character, that person is free to operate freely, regardless of civil laws or company policies. I knew, therefore, that unfairness was bound to come. Commitment and hard work were my only safeguards.

Then came a major weather disaster that affected Detroit, and I was called in to work. I worked throughout the night hoping to be allowed to stay home with my family the next day, which was a holiday. But duty called. I worked for two days, almost nonstop. When I submitted my time card for pay, the supervisor in charge would only pay me for half the hours that I worked. I believed that she was following a cue from Janet, who was away on vacation. It was blatantly unfair, but I choose not to argue.

A few days after the incident, the company announced that employees would get an additional lump sum payment if they had worked more than a certain number of hours during the emergency. I fit the criteria according to my calculations but not according to the way my time had been entered. Again, I approached the supervisor in charge and asked that my time be corrected. She refused, saying that she did not believe I had worked all the hours reported. She demanded proof. I asked if the other employees who worked during the emergency had to provide proof. When she said no, I felt oppressed and harassed. I resisted feeling resentful, but I was determined to get all of the money that was owed me.

I found another supervisor who approved my adjustment, and I sent my time card in for processing. Within two days, a manager called the Pay Department to hold my request for the correction. The department held my adjustment and secretly placed me under investigation for falsely reporting hours and stealing from the company. They had not yet received the computerized report of hours worked during the emergency, but they chose to consider me guilty until proven innocent. Later, I learned that the supervisor in charge spoke negatively about me, influencing the investigation. When Janet returned from vacation, she quickly sided with the supervisor in charge.

7: Harassment at Every Turn

After two weeks the computerized reports confirmed the time I had worked during the emergency, except for one hour, and that hour was easily clarified. The dispatcher deactivated my working status as soon as he dispatched my relief person, not taking into account that I had to wait an hour until my relief arrived. I refused to sign the time card until I got everything that was due me. When the problem was finally resolved and the records confirmed my whereabouts, I did not get an apology from any of the perpetrators.

And ye shall know the truth, and the truth shall make you free.
John 8:32

As I look back now, I realize that harassment had started within six months of my joining the Marketing department.

I remember one very busy day, when I was rushing to complete my last task during the 25 minutes remaining before 5 p.m. Suddenly a supervisor came from behind, grabbed me round the waist and said, "I would like to put you on the table and keep you there until 5:30." Then he scurried away. Although I was the victim, I put myself on trial, asking what had prompted this action? I never flirted. I never wore revealing shirts that showed cleavage. I never made myself available to him. Perhaps this was a test to see how far he could go. Was it a coincidence that this man was a very close friend of Trace. I found myself innocent of any potential charges, and I reported the event to my director. Although, my director and the perpetrator were close friends, there was an immediate response to my concern, and the offender was ordered to apologize. Looking back now, I

7: Harassment at Every Turn

realize how important it is to report harassment immediately. When I did, as in this incident, I stopped the problem before it got out of hand.

The harassment continued during the period when I was still confident about my career. I remember being asked to attend a two-day seminar in Ohio, which sounded like acceptance of my professional abilities. When I told my husband about the seminar, he shared my excitement and wished me well. Traveling to the event with other marketing representatives, account representatives and potential customers was wonderful. Everyone was carefree and relaxed.

After several hours of travel, we arrived at our destination in time for a late lunch where people chatted and socialized. I noticed that Spikey, one of the marketing executives and a good friend of Clara's, seemed extremely friendly. He stayed close to me from the moment we arrived, through class sessions and a tour of the facility. After the day's activities, we were escorted to a room where finger foods and alcoholic beverages were served. I indulged in a soda and some snacks and began chatting with Percillia. Spikey joined us and then Canaan. Canaan knew my husband and wanted to know how he was doing, but when I responded, Spikey became loud and abusive about my husband.

I did not understand his behavior. How could someone who did not know anything about my husband have such strong feelings against him? I had no answers. After this cocktail hour, we boarded the bus to our hotel. As we were checking in, Spikey approached me with firm instructions to be at the bar by 8 p.m. that evening. I felt very reluctant to comply because I am a born-again Christian, I am married and I did not appreciate the commotion that had taken place at the social gathering. I began to suspect other reasons for why I was invited on the trip. I went to my room and decided to stay there for the evening, amusing myself with television and radio. When I came down to breakfast the next morning, Spikey was furious. He said, "Sharon, I can't believe you stayed in your room all night. We are going to put you behind a computer screen and leave you there. You are not going anywhere in the company because of the way you are."

Later that day, he asked me some technical questions about the seminar we attended. When I answered them, Spikey commented that I learned quickly but couldn't read the signs. Later he added that I did not know how men think. Only then did I realize that the trip was not intended to be a learning experience but rather an opportunity for sexual pleasures. Thank God I did not go to the bar that night. When we boarded the bus for home, Spikey seemed on the verge of violence. When he stared me down, I looked out of the window. Then an account representative who had worked on a project with me bragged that Spikey was going to promote him. Jokingly, I said that I should get a promotion as well. In an angry voice, Spikey shouted repeatedly, "Sharon, what are you going to do for me?" All of the people on the bus were silenced because they knew that he was blatantly referring to sexual favors in exchange.

Looking up into the blue, clear skies and the bright sun, I wondered how to get out of this situation. I wanted to report him, but I didn't, feeling indebted to him because of past work. I also did not want to be considered a tattletale.

But I was wrong not to report him. Later, he committed worse offenses, spreading rumors throughout the company that I was a lesbian and urging colleagues to torment me. Only when things got completely out of control, did I report him to the manager. Then I discovered that he had never respected me as a team player or even a human. I allowed myself to suffer great persecution to save a business relationship and a career opportunity that did not exist.

*I will stand upon my watch and set me upon the tower, and
will see what he will say unto me . . .*

Habakkuk 2:1

There were times when I worried, cried and even
questioned GOD. "Why me?"

I had proven myself a professional and a team
player. All my efforts were directed to being accepted by
the executives in Marketing. My bedroom floor was
carpeted with charts, graphs and analyses, as I strove to
be the "best" in my field. Where I fell short of knowledge, my husband offered his professional advice. I also
had friends who supported me. Night after night I
labored, planting the seeds and watching others harvest
the fruit. No matter how hard I tried to be recognized for
my efforts and be promoted, others were promoted over
me while I stayed at the same level. Someone in Marketing always ask me to do most of the work, but the
promotions and the salary increases went elsewhere. I
was never asked to lead, just to follow.

I needed to know why, and one night the answer
came. I dreamed that a co-worker and I were assigned to
inspect a large vacant apartment building. It was four
stories high and had 12 apartments on each floor. We
began on the first floor where the apartments were in
excellent condition; then we moved to the second floor.
Surprisingly, the second floor was also in good condition; there were only one or two cracks in the walls that
needed to be caulked. The third floor needed more
repairs, painting, toilet repairs and new carpeting. But
on the fourth and last level, there were even more repairs
needed. We recorded all the repairs that were needed,
and then we opened the door to the last apartment. I

went in a back room and noticed a trap door to an attic from which blood was seeping out. Immediately, I called my co-worker, and he determined to inspect the attic. He went to his van to retrieve a special one-piece silver suit that had a head piece, enclosed gloves and boots. When he returned, he grabbed a ladder to climb through the small door. I wanted to go along, but I did not have the proper gear. Eagerly, I watched him climb the ladder. Moments later, he peered down through the trap door and said, "Sharon you cannot come up here because it is too contaminated." The dream ended there.

Immediately I woke up, I felt sad because I knew what the dream meant. The first two floors of the apartment represented my work environment while I was in clerical positions. There were no temptations or competition when I was a typist. Even as a semi-professional, I experienced no real problems, and I was never expected to compromise my values. However, as I gained a more professional position, there were more temptations, and I felt less respect for my values. I believe the small attic personified the highest ranking officers of my company, which included only a select few. The blood seeping through the trap door and running down the walls signified a corrupt environment where some executives in upper management consistently cut the throats of others to maintain their status.

The next day, I put on my Sunday best and went to church. It was a wonderful service, where I received confirmation about my dream. That day, the Pastor preached about contamination and God's warning that we can not allow certain things to destroy our relationship with God. Listening to the sermon, I thought about the dream, about the compromising and the politics that seems to be a way of life in the corporation. There was a decision to be made; I had to choose between God and my career. Nothing would separate me from the love of God. God did not choose my career in Marketing; I had chosen it for myself, without God's approval.

I was put in the headquarters of hell for three years, where I worked with followers of the occult and the new age movement. I was used as an instrument to tear down the Devil's kingdom. My purpose was to beat down the establishment, to weaken them and scatter them so that other innocent people would not be destroyed by the same evil workers. I felt the pain of threshing down their high places; I felt the pressure until I realized that God was using me for his purpose.

Courage

There shall not any man be able to stand before thee all the days of thy life. As I was with Moses, so I will be with thee. I will not fail thee nor forsake thee. Be strong and of a good courage: for unto this people shalt thou divide for an inheritance the land, which I swore unto their fathers to give them.

Joshua 1:5-6

I had tried many times to resolve my problems through supervisor, director, manager and human resource coordinator. My supervisor was not one to discuss unfairness, but I had two short meetings with my director, three long meetings with the human resource coordinator and one meeting with the manager. All efforts were unsuccessful. I was still being harassed.

I felt oppressed and cornered by corrupted authorities with no way out. My physical health and mental health could not take any more pressure. If I could not resolve the problem within the company, I could go to the Equal Employment Opportunity Commission for assistance. This was the hardest decision I ever made. Going to an outside agency meant acknowledging a major problem, and there was a sense of shame and dishonor associated with this experience. I would have to reveal my actual experiences and after working 20 years for the company, I felt as if I was betraying everyone.

Then, I realized there was no alternative. Only government intervention could stop the harassment and the conspiracy because the situation had no internal resolution. On a bright summer day in August, 1992, I walked through the busy streets of downtown Detroit to the EEOC, talking courage into myself. Repeatedly, I would say, "They left me no choice; no one there cares; I have to do what I have to do."

I walked to the Federal Building in a state of panic. By the time I entered the building, I was numb from my worries and concerns. But when I entered the elevator and pushed the button to the 6th floor, everything went blank. I shed everything in that elevator. Entering the office, courage came; the courage that enables one to face danger or hardship with confidence and resolution seemed to rise within me. By the time I walked through the doors of the Equal Employment Opportunity Commission, I was confident of my decision. I signed in at the reception's desk without reservation. Help was only moments away.

9: Counsel and Encouragement

Ointment and perfume rejoice the heart: so doth the sweetness of a man's friends by hearty counsel.

Proverbs 27:9

And the people, the men of Israel, encouraged themselves, and set their battle again in array in the place where they put themselves in array the first day.

Judges 20:22

The pressure did not end after I started proceedings with the EEOC. Sometimes I was so mentally and physically drained by the end of the day that I wondered how long I could hold out. It was devastating to experience harassment and be ignorant of why it was happening, how many were involved in the conspiracy, or how it would affect me and my career. There were many times when I wanted to run away from it all but I couldn't because my tribulations allowed me to be counted worthy of the kingdom of God. My character of enduring hardship and suffering was being developed. Frankly I could not have overcome my hardship without God's power and strength. I received comfort and consolation from spiritual leaders, loved ones, friends, scriptures and fellow Christians. Wise counsel brought light to my darkness. Words of encouragement motivated me to see it through.

Faith coupled with understanding enabled me to be steadfast and unmovable. In the darkest moments of my career, God's Word kept me alive. I attended bible class and held onto the words that never changed, that could never be altered by man. God's word that will stand forever allowed me to overcome every situation. Where others had nervous breakdowns, heart attacks or lost hope and gave up the battle, God would not let me run,

9: Counsel and Encouragement

nor hide but he made me face my enemies.

The Pastor and Co-pastor of my church were fiery but filled with the joy and energy of the Lord. Although, they were loving Christians, they believed in upholding righteousness at whatever cost. They were fearless, spiritual warriors who believed that Satan and all of his evil workers could be defeated by Christians. Many times, I would enter the church exhausted and down-trodden only to receive their wise counsel and experi-ence a spiritual renewal. Like boxing coaches, they patched me up and sent me back into the ring for the next round. Tirelessly, they prayed day and night for me and had faith that I would eventually give them a good report.

In the depths of my disappointments, the Holy Scriptures comforted and strengthened me. There were personal messages that helped me mature through terrible persecutions, given directly from God, preached from the pulpit or delivered by fellow Christians. I regained hope every time I saw the unchangeable prom-ises of victory in God's holy word because the words gave me an understanding of God's plan. I was going through a painful experience, but I was under the juris-diction of Jesus Christ, who gave me victory in every situation.

I was surrounded by enemies, persecuted at one time by five people. The harassments were verbal, sexual and designed to cause me mental anguish, but regardless of what was said and done, I never lost a battle. God fought with me. One by one, my tormentors began to have problems at home. One experienced a terrible divorce, another was diagnosed with a brain tumor, a third had to work at home for two months because of personal problems. God dealt with one after the other right before my eyes, but did they understand why? I asked God to show them why they were being judged and to save them.

My husband who supervised engineers, counseled me on how to use the employee grievance procedure. He told me what resources were available to me inside and outside the company, and he warned me how to recognize when trouble came. For example, I noticed that they were daily taking away my responsibilities until I had nothing to do. My husband told me to go immediately to the director and request work. I took my husband's advice. When I asked the director for work, he told me that I was moving to another location and assuming different duties. But, in the meantime, the director gave me some meaningful work to do. It was a major victory.

I also had the comfort and counsel of friends who came to the office to see me. They helped me laugh in the midst of my persecutions, and I was strengthened by the laughter. One young man seemed to radiate confidence and strength though he was humble and soft spoken. When he visited me, it seemed that all my enemies scattered. Other Christians who worked with me shared my load; some shared scriptures, while others ministered to me in prayer. Words cannot express how valuable these people were to me not just because of their wise counsel but for their physical presence in my times of need.

9: Counsel and Encouragement

Tenacious
Wherefore take unto you the whole armor of God, that ye may be able to withstand in the evil day, and having done all, to stand.

Stand therefore, having your loins girt about with truth and having on the breastplate of righteousness.
Ephesians 6:13-14

Daily, my father insisted that I stand fast and not make it easy for my enemies. "We've got to persevere," he said. As an example, he told me of an experience he had when he became a foreman. His boss was a prejudiced man, determined to fire my father. Day after day the boss built up the pressure until my father left. A week after my father quit, the man died. After his retirement, my father was still talking about what he could have been if he had only hung in there.

Too often, we advise our friends and children not to put up with the hard knocks. We tell others that once they get a college education they won't "have to take anything from anybody," and that is not true. One of my best friends obtained a Master's degree in computer science. As a minority with a degree, she was always in demand. But everywhere she worked, people harassed her because of her Christian principles. She quit all of her good jobs, until eventually she settled for a job that required no degree. Her salary was low, and she was always scumming around borrowing money for rent.

It is not convenient to have to deal with harassment and stand to see the end. But I realized that I was standing up for a principle, and I had to stand fast. I remember watching interviews with the referees before the

9: Counsel and Encouragement

Holyfield-Tyson fight. Tyson didn't want a certain referee because the man had made calls that Tyson disagreed with. As a result the referee resigned from the fight. A prominent man who was being interviewed by a reporter about the resignation had this to say:

"The whole situation is very unfortunate. I personally know the referee is a good man, but he must learn to live life. I strongly disagree with the resignation because the judges never voted him out, and the owners never thought about voting him out. Frankly, if it were me and they lit sticks of dynamite and blew the place up – by God I would still be standing. I would not resign from my job and lose all of my money, but he's got to learn. He must learn how to take the knocks of life because no matter what call you make somebody will always refute you. Somebody will always second guess your ability."

That speech hit home with me.

I remembered one boss I had who worked his way up through the ranks of the company, which increased his job knowledge and enabled him to become sensitive to people. He had an engineering degree and then worked to obtain a law degree in his later years with the company. He fought to implement programs for the betterment of the company, enduring heated confrontations with his peers. When he finally became a manager, I thought that his struggle was over. I visited him to inquire about his progress only to learn that the fight, the struggle and the second guessing from his peers continued even at his new level in management.

10: Fighting Harassment

And whatsoever ye do in word or deed, do all in the name of the Lord Jesus, giving thanks to God and the Father by him.
Colossians 3:17

Servants, obey in all things your masters according to the flesh; not with eye service, as men pleasers, but in singleness of heart fearing God.

And whatsoever ye do, do it heartily, as to the Lord, and not unto men.

Knowing that of the Lord ye shall receive the reward of the inheritance, for ye serve the Lord Christ.
Colossians 3:22-24

It is almost impossible to withstand the pressures of harassment. The sooner you choose to deal with the problem the better it will be for you mentally and physically. Start resisting harassment by being aware of your abilities and being secure about your skills and professionalism. Note those talents and abilities that are natural, and promote the skills, abilities and talents you have inherited. Ask God about your career and what is best for you. I believe that what a man soweth, he shall reap. At the same time, be alert to your environment to note treatment that may ultimately cause you harm. Compare your treatment and job status with that of your peers to note differences in relationships or in promotions, but do not look to the opinions of others to validate your worth.

How believable you are depends on your record. Daily assignments are measures of credibility, showing a consistent track record of good attendance and good performance. Maintain good work records and try to earn certificates and awards that prove your accomplishments. These life-long records will reveal who you are and record your contributions to the company. Selection committees rarely take chances on hiring people who do not possess references and credentials. In corporations, many people believe what they hear and only half of what they see. Therefore, credibility must be proven at every point in time and for every project. You must work with a purpose to establish credibility. One of the major factors in establishing credibility is doing what is right, which should not depend on your relationship with your boss.

In the event that bad situations develop between you and your boss continue to show kindness, follow through on all of your boss' requests and remain accessible. Implement your duties with diligence when your boss is away from the office. Continue to perform your duties to the best of your ability if you receive an unfair evaluation. Be enthusiastic about each assignment. Keep in mind that someone is always watching you, evaluating you and determining whether you are dependable and promotable. In these days, integrity is priceless in the work place. Do your job, and your efforts will pay off.

Get enthusiastic about your work, and take pride in doing it well. Always maintain a level of professionalism on the job. It is so important to perform to the best of your ability, to adhere to a work schedule and to get a record of positive statements about your performance for your files. Be conscientious about when you start and how long you take for breaks or lunch. Get cross-functional work assignments or assignments that expose you to other areas of the company. Don't depend on people from your immediate department to take you to the next level. Sell yourself to other departments. Follow instructions and add more information to your reports and work; this shows that you have intentions to satisfy your customers. Your proaction is invaluable because so many workers have not been taught how to provide quality service and add value to the company.

At the same time, understand that you have the right to work in an environment free from harassment, discrimination and intimidation. One problem we all have is giving the perpetrator the benefit of the doubt, hoping that if we ignore the harassment the problem will end. Unfortunately, ignoring harassment empowers the perpetrator to continue at the expense of your mental, physical and spiritual well being. If you experience harassment and discrimination, immediately tell the person who is harassing you to stop the unwelcome behavior. Be candid and direct and immediately warn the harasser that if the behavior continues you will report it to a supervisor or Human Resources. If there is repeated unwelcome behavior, follow through on your warning.

In my experience, there are always signs, warnings and hints of breakdowns in business relationships. The first sign is generally a breakdown in communication, which requires willing and open parties working together. Good communications are essential to all relationships whether at work, home or church. They involve giving good instructions, listening attentively to the given instructions, repeating the instructions in your own words to clarify the facts, following through on your commitment to effectively complete the assignment and immediately reporting pertinent events that may affect the progress of the assignment.

10: Fighting Harassment

Communications are faulty when your supervisor frequently gives you incorrect information about your assignments so you are redoing work unnecessarily, or the supervisor waits until the last minute to give information for the assignment and you rush to meet an impossible deadline making errors in the process. These are subtle forms of harassment that create hardship, stress, frustration and embarrassment. Pay attention to the signs of deteriorating business relations, and take charge with open, frequent and positive communications. During meetings, always focus on the common goals of an assignment, getting as much information as you can and using your ingenuity to determine what would make the job more complete. Tell your supervisor if a job may not be completed within the deadline because of the short time frame given to complete the job. At the same time, do everything possible to complete it within the allotted time. Stay in control of your time by stating the priorities and estimating completion. Mention that in the future you would appreciate ample notice of assignments and realistic deadlines so that you can efficiently complete assignments. Document these instances when you have one-on-one reviews.

Move quickly to resolve problems when they arise, and report incidents to the proper authorities. Consistency in work relationships is essential to right dealings with others. The moment you deviate from consistency, whether you are a victim or not, you are guilty of discrimination. Go forward by faith and when you reach your destination, courage will surely come. Make your supervisor aware of the harassment, and report all details, no matter how shameful. This is not simply an option; it is your responsibility. You owe it to your boss or superior to quickly resolve a problem. Do not be concerned about your reputation or how this could hinder future opportunities. These harassers also report to a higher authority, and it's up to you to uncover the problem. Most of the time, you are not the only victim. As soon as you make the incident known, other victims may surface or you may find that yours is an incident that is being added to an established track record of this type of behavior.

I've learned to face problems directly. When trouble comes, I've asked my boss to call all of the perpetrators into the office with myself. This has stopped many potential problems in the early stages of development.

A verbal report is sufficient to start with because time is of the essence. When confronting the harasser, resist negative remarks. Instead state why you are concerned with the harasser's behavior. Talk about your strengths with pride, and mention the harasser's shortcomings with boldness, but speak in love and truth. You must also work harder to demonstrate your strengths and talents. Be creative, always adding more than what has been offered to be proactive.

Defensive positioning is an effective technique which can stop most harassment. Know the hierarchy of the organization and the names of the senior executives. Choose your moment carefully, and then make your senior officer aware of the problem. When you plead your case, describe the situation in detail and explain how the harassment hinders fairness and productivity in the workplace. More and more companies are hiring ombudspersons who serve as mediators to resolve

10: Fighting Harassment

problems before litigation. You will get results when you are right and when you approach the authority who can get results.

Write a letter to your manager and provide details: actual words used, time of the incident and place. Tell the truth, the whole truth and nothing but the truth because only truth will correct the act and make you free.

Documentation is a necessary tool for your survival in the corporate world. It captures the pattern and reveals the plans of the offenders. If the harasser is a supervisor using subtle techniques of harassment, protect yourself by getting as much information as possible. Ask questions about each assignment:

- What is the purpose/objective of the assignment?
- What are the instructions?
- When is it due?
- How do I begin?
- Who else is involved?
- Is there a special format?

Document assignments, instructions, date requested, date given, dated required and the requestor. Note any unusual events. These notes will help support your case, by identifying the trends and methods of the harassers. As part of your documentation, keep a work journal, noting job opportunities missed. If harassment starts, maintain the journal daily, logging assignments started and completed, instructions and changes in instructions, unusual occurrences or miscommunications. Document all events in a story form with a narrative, describing all significant events and offenses. Reviewing the journal weekly will alert you to situations that require immediate reporting. You can study your mistakes, develop a strategy and determine how to overcome the situation.

Unfortunately, notes are just evidence of one person's word against another person. It's therefore helpful to keep other evidence such as email or computerized messages. Make sure you have such evidence by requesting email instructions and scheduling a meeting by email to discuss the project in detail.

Sometimes it is also important to tape meetings.

Often men are stereotyped as the harassers because most reported instances are sexual in nature, but women can and do harass other women. Clara was a female harasser. She humiliated me before other professionals, discredited my work and lied on my appraisals. I had reported her actions, but no one seemed to care. I had documented every assignment and every action, but words could not describe her harassment. I needed to describe her voice and her tone when she spoke to me as if I was less than human and unworthy of my rightful place. Then, I received the answer: A tape recorder would describe the voice, stress, confrontation, and dehumanization that she initiated. Such documentation would relieve me of any further questions.

As I entered her office with my portfolio, the attacks immediately began. While giving me her instructions, she was extremely hostile. I was never allowed to finished my sentences. There were constant and unnecessary confrontations, but I sat calmly for the tape to capture the moment. It was better than a Kodak moment. After, 30 minutes of this treatment, I managed to get the assignment and leave the office. I gave a copy of the tape to the vice president to let him hear the harassment that I

10: Fighting Harassment

had experienced. He would not have believed what had just taken place if I had not taped it.

To prepare for taping, proceed as follows:

- Purchase a microcassette recorder and 60-minute microcassettes.
- Test your recorder to ensure that the voices are distinguishable.
- Test the batteries to ensure that there is enough power to tape the proceedings.
- Time yourself to determine when the tape is completed and ask to leave the room when you need to turn the tape or change cassettes.
- Label the taped conversations and store them in a safe place.

During a taped session, remain calm and exhibit normal behavior. Do not let your harasser know about the taping. Let the harasser know that you find the comments uncomfortable or offensive, and state that you wish them to end.

When facing these trials, you need courage to conquer your deepest fears. Courage defeats all odds, and courage strengthens. You must have courage to overcome harassment in the work place. Without courage you may waver and fear the repercussions of the oppressors. Too often, we concern ourselves with secondary issues: What will people say or think? How will this impact my future?

To meet the challenge and conquer the oppressor is a fearless endeavor. Courage relieves sleepless nights where worry has interfered with your sleep. It facilitates your plans to implement quick resolutions. It's a promise that no man will be able to stand before you when you execute your plans and demand that harassment cease. Courage is a stop sign to those who have been on "go" and have not been refuted. Courage is anticipating the battle because after the battle you can receive the blessings and ultimately gain your rightful place. Deal with the problem and the harasser – one on one, or even one on ten.

Get counsel from those who are close to you. Don't internalize your feelings of defeat and depression. Let them know what is happening so that you can get the right instruction. Soon help will come.

11: What To Do, Where To Go

Even so faith, if it hath not works, is dead, being alone.

James 2:17

When channels within the company are not effective, it is time to try an outside agency. The Equal Employment Opportunities Commission enforces Title VII of the Civil Rights Act of 1964, the Age Discrimination in Employment Act of 1967, the Equal Pay Act of 1963, Title I of the Americans with Disabilities Act of 1990, and the Civil Rights Act of 1991. You must file charges in person or by mail within a specified time from the alleged discriminatory act. The date of filing ranges from 180 to 300 days, according to the mandate of the agency in your state.

The EEOC processes the charge and sends the company notification of the charge, which is received by the Director of Employee Relations. A human resources consultant is assigned to investigate the charge and notifies your work area, which must answer the allegations. The EEOC investigator reviews your allegations and management's response and may request a resolution conference to discuss the facts surrounding the allegations. The conference, which can take one to three hours, is attended by the human resource consultant, a representative from management, usually the supervisor, the claimant and the investigator who conducts the meeting. Following the conference, the agency issues a determination, but this process can take up to two years. After the issuance of the determination, the case is closed, but the charge remains in the company's files indefinitely. The Michigan Department of Civil Rights handles charges similarly.

11: What To Do, Where To Go

The EEOC uses alternative dispute resolution to resolve disputes without litigation through such means as arbitration and negotiation, which are effective in eliminating work place discrimination. The particular form of ADR that has been adopted by the Commission is facilitative mediation, an informal negotiation process where the parties are guided toward a settlement of their dispute by a trained mediator who has no ties to either side. The setting in which mediation takes place is informal, nonadversarial and confidential, and the program is voluntary for all parties. With the assistance of the mediator, each party has an opportunity to tell its side of the story without interruption. The mediator helps the parties identify the issues and create options for solving them, encouraging discussion. If the parties have a technical question about the laws that EEOC enforces and about EEOC charge processing procedures, they can ask. The individual who responds to the request does not give advice on the worth of a case or the terms of a settlement. Charges are held in the mediation program for a maximum of 90 days; then they are forwarded to the investigative division for normal charge processing.

If the charge is not settled through mediation, it is forwarded to a unit for investigation and assigned in the order it was originally received. In other words, the charge does not lose its "place in line" as a penalty for having gone through mediation. If the dispute is not resolved through mediation and investigation, there is always litigation.

Be proactive; don't wait until the last moment to prepare for possible legal action. Schedule annual legal consultations with a legal service, a group of attorneys

11: What To Do, Where To Go

who specialize in certain areas of the law like discrimination, or with an attorney who specializes in employment law. Here are some guidelines to follow to assure that you have the best legal representation:

1. Make a list of attorneys who are knowledgeable about employment law and have been recommended.
2. Research your list to determine their track records.
3. Prioritize your list based on the findings.
4. Schedule appointments with the attorney to discuss the details of your case. Don't be discouraged if the attorney rejects your case, just continue your research. That attorney is not confident of your chances of winning, and most attorneys will not pursue your case if it is not an easy win.
5. Select the best attorney for you.
6. Establish regular communications with your attorney by phone and in person. Make the first office visit a productive one by having all of your research at hand.
7. Document all pertinent events for your attorney's review.

Signs of a good attorney are as follows:

1. The attorney takes a personal interest in your case.
2. The attorney provides a clear sense of direction, legal advice and adequate feedback on the first visit without money up front.
3. The attorney is thorough about the details of your case.
4. The attorney returns your phone calls.

11: What To Do, Where To Go

During the negotiation and legal process, continue to perform to the best of your ability and keep a positive attitude. Tell yourself that you have the victory, that you will make it through these times, and that you will not allow your harassers to dominate your thoughts. There will be times when it will seem like you are alone but you must stand with courage and faith that with God's help you will overcome the harassment. Be patient and you will make it through victoriously.

Be assured that the word of God will stand forever. Let thy mercies come also unto me, O Lord, even thy salvation according to thy word. So shall I have wherewith to answer him that reproaches me. I trust in thy word.

Psalms 119:41-42

Scripture inspired me throughout my severe persecutions.

When harassment, discrimination and hardships occur, it is important that we understand what's happening to handle situations better. God uses us as instruments to destroy spiritual wickedness. An instrument has no control of the task at hand. Only, the master makes a decision about which tool best fits the purpose to complete the task. As instruments, we feel the pain of execution; we feel the threshing and beating. But if we understand our place and stay in the spirit, the pain will lessen because we are assured that we will not be defeated when God is doing the work.

Behold, I will make thee a new sharp threshing instrument having teeth. Thou shalt thresh the mountains, and beat them small, and shall make the hills as chaff. Thou shalt fan them, and the wind shall carry them away and the whirlwind shall scatter them, and thou shalt rejoice in the Lord and shalt glory in the Holy One of Israel.

Isaiah 41:15-16

In place of David's name, insert your own. Pray to see the manifestation of the Word of God. God keeps his word, do you have the faith to believe him?

12: Keeping The Faith

*I have found David my servant; with my holy oil have I
anointed him. With whom my hand shall be established; mine
arm also shall strengthen him. The enemy shall not exact upon
him; nor the son of wickedness afflict him. And I will beat
down his foes before his face, and plague them that hate him.*
Psalms 89:20-24

Be not fearful despite the false accusations, harassments and even discrimination. Let joy radiate forth,
strengthening you to overcome your hardship. You
cannot let anyone take your joy. Joy allows you to draw
from your well of salvation, the well God has given us
that supplies us with everything. Joy is what draws the
living water.

*Behold, God is my salvation; I will trust, and not be afraid, for
the Lord Jehovah is my strength and my song; he also is
become my salvation.*

*Therefore with joy shall ye draw water out of the wells of
salvation.*
Isaiah 12:2-3

God anticipates an uproar when he places us
amongst evil doers. In fact, the scripture indicates that
God starts trouble to destroy oppression. We are not to
worry about the weapons used, whether sexual harassment, discrimination, or blackballing, because they will
not prosper. Evil workers are going to gather together
against us, but they will not have God's approval to
destroy the believer.

*Behold, they shall surely gather together, but not by me.
Whosoever shall gather together against thee shall fall for thy*
sake.

Behold, I have created the smith that bloweth the coals in the fire, and that bringeth forth an instrument for his work. I have created the waster to destroy.

No weapon that is formed against thee shall prosper . . .
Isaiah 54:15-17

After the grace period, God deals with your enemies before your eyes.

Behold, a whirlwind of the Lord is gone forth in fury, even a grievous whirlwind. It shall fall grievously upon the head of the wicked. The anger of the Lord shall not return, until he have executed, and till he have performed the thoughts of his heart. In the latter days, ye shall consider it perfectly.
Jeremiah 23:19-20

Did you know that the wicked man has a portion and a heritage appointed unto him by God?

Because he hath oppressed and hath forsaken the poor; because he hath violently taken away a house which he builded not. Surely he shall not feel quietness in his belly, he shall not save of that which he desired.

All darkness shall be hid in his secret places. A fire not blown shall consume him; it shall go ill with him that is left in his tabernacle. The heaven shall reveal his iniquity, and the earth shall rise up against him.
Job 20:19-20, 26-27

When you want God to finish the battle – call on Sabaoth, the Lord of Hosts. He comes as a warrior to fight the battle. He comes with whatever it takes to win the battle. Get to know the Christians who work in your department and in the company so that you can spiritually support each other. Know that you are never alone, but the Lord of Host "Sabaoth" is with you and will deliver you.

Behold, the hire of the laborers who have reaped down your fields, which is of you kept back by fraud, crieth; and the cries of them which have reaped are entered into the ears of the Lord of Sabaoth.

James 5:4

God through His Son Jesus Christ has given us power over harassment, racism, persecution and all evil. Evil shall not hurt us.

Behold, I give you power to tread on serpents and scorpions, and over all the power of the enemy, and nothing shall by any means hurt you.

Luke 10:19

There is no need to worry about the devices of the heathen. God is a refuge and a fortress, and He protects the righteous in every situation. Remind God about his promises. Command the Scripture to come alive.

The Lord bringeth the counsel of the heathen to nought. He make the devices of the people of none effect. The counsel of the Lord standeth for ever, the thoughts of his heart to all generations.

Psalms 33:10-11

12: Keeping The Faith

Millions of people are destroyed through harassment and discrimination because of the fear that is generated. Fear is the strength of the devil. It takes your joy, paralyzes and overwhelms your mind so that you cannot think clearly or act rationally. God gives us love and faith to conquer evil. You cannot hate your enemy and expect to overcome harassment; you cannot use the same weapon (hate) that your oppressor uses. God has also given you a sound mind to focus on His goodness and His purpose for you in this test.

For God hath not given us the spirit of fear; but of power, and of love and of a sound mind.

II Timothy 1:7

The Lord gives righteous judgment, and all men shall receive their right reward from God. God is willing that none should perish, even those who discriminated, harassed and verbally abused you. He encourages the Christian to stay on the righteous path, and be assured that God ordered our footsteps to this trial to make us strong. When we delight ourselves in the Lord, he will give us the desires of our hearts. No man can take your blessings from you, but you can give them away and even miss God's blessings by being envious and carnal.

Fret not thyself because of evildoers, neither be thou envious against the workers of iniquity.

For they shall soon be cut down like the grass, and wither as the green herb.

I have seen the wicked in great power, and spreading himself like a green bay tree.

12: Keeping The Faith

Yet he passed away, and lo, he was not. Yea, I sought him, but he could not be found.

Psalms 37:1-2, 35-36

We should not be frightened when our enemies harass us because God causes them to come against us to bring them down and to scatter them. Know His divine plan, understand your heritage. The heathen will not rule over you. Christians who obey God cannot go wrong.

The Lord shall cause thine enemies that rise up against thee to be smitten before thy face. They shall come out against thee one way and flee before thee seven ways.

And the Lord shall make thee the head and not the tail, and thou shalt be above only, and thou shalt not be beneath. If that thou hearken unto the commandments of the Lord thy God, which I command thee this day, to observe and to do them.

Deuteronomy 28:7-13

It is possible to have victory in your situation. No matter who the perpetrator is or what you have gone through, there is hope in Christ Jesus. God can rescue you.

For whatsoever is born of God overcometh the world, and this is the victory that overcometh the world, even our faith.

Who is he that overcometh the world, but he that believeth that Jesus is the Son of God?

1 John 5:4-5

12: Keeping The Faith

You can become one of His people by receiving Jesus Christ as your Lord and Savior. You must be born again to possess the promises, but don't come just for the promises. Come because He is a Savior and a Deliverer. Come because you want to get to heaven.

Except a man be born again, he cannot see the kingdom of God, nor can he possess the promises.

John 3:3

Repent of your sins and ask Him to cleanse you from all unrighteousness.

I tell you, nay. But, except ye repent, ye shall all likewise perish.

Luke 13:3

Confess your sins to God and ask forgiveness.

If we confess our sins, he is faithful and just to forgive us our sins, and to cleanse us from all unrighteousness.

I John 1:9

God will not condemn you for past sins, he will forgive if you CONFESS today.

That if thou shalt confess with thy mouth the Lord Jesus, and shalt believe in thine heart that God hath raised him from the dead, thou shalt be saved.

For with the heart man believeth unto righteousness, and with the mouth confession is made unto salvation.

Romans 10:9-10

. . . forgetting those things which are behind, and reaching forth unto those things which are before, I press toward the mark for the prize of the high calling of God in Christ Jesus.
Philippians 3:13-14

Recovery means restoring oneself to a normal state. That's what happened to me. I was transferred to another building and department after my life was threatened and did not have any direct contact with the perpetrators. Gradually, I assumed a different posture – one of authority, positiveness and joy. Separation from the environment and the passage of time allowed me to heal from the hurts of the past. The moment that I was able to leave job matters at the work place recovery began, and I obtained peace of mind. Renewal of mind, body and soul is the most important component of recovery.

When trouble and disappointment comes in our lives, it is normal to hurt, but we must remember that it is also normal to heal. Healing is a natural process that comes with time. However, we can impede the healing progress by constantly rethinking and reliving our negative experiences. When we concentrate on the details of bad experiences, it's like opening an old wound. We choose to be engulfed in the wrong that we have suffered.

Recovery starts in the mind. Remember bad experiences to learn life's valuable lessons, but don't let those bad experiences take over your life. You can stop harassment and go on with your life. However, it is impossible to recover when negative experiences are constantly on your mind. You must think positively and cherish the good things of life: your children and grandchildren,

13: Recovery

your husband, your health, your godly sisters and
brothers, your ability and strength in Christ Jesus.

*... whatsoever things are true, whatsoever things are honest,
whatsoever things are just, whatsoever things are lovely and of
a good report, if there be any virtue and praise, think on these
things.*

Philippians 4:8

Attitude is everything. Guard against belligerence,
hostility and negativity. Don't let hardships pull you
down, and don't let your mind rest in negative places.
Elevate your thoughts so that you and your loved ones
can begin to heal and enjoy life. I think that a sign posted
in my beauty shop sums it up: "Lord, let my setbacks be
my comebacks."

Although being persecuted on the job is an obstacle
to your career and your physical being, you can make a
comeback. Let your hardship be a springboard to a
higher position in the work place. Don't give up on your
career or your aspirations. Determine that you will get
something out of the negative experience. Determine
that you will not be defeated and reach above and
beyond discrimination, harassment and verbal abuse.
Take this opportunity to bid for higher paying jobs. Go
to college for higher education; begin new hobbies; use
your skills to help those in need. Forward thinking helps
the recovery process because your positive energy and
focus are on personal achievements which are always
rewarding. Visualize yourself stepping over the obstacle
to a higher level and do it!!! No matter what disappointments you experience, don't give up. You are closer to
your goal than you think.

I remember one young man who exemplified this positive attitude. He joined the company as an entry level customer representative and then was fired for some medical reason despite his being extremely pleasant and working well with others. I thought it a shame, until I met him one year later at a gas station. He told me that one week after he was fired, the company he and his brother had founded was awarded a $1 million contract from the government to install fire hydrants in low income housing. He said that although the company fired him, he kept thinking positively and believing that opportunities would be available to him if he kept the faith. We rejoiced and I wished him well. Then I returned to my car and meditated on the goodness of God during the darkest moments.

One sign of recovery is forgiveness. Forgiveness does not mean opening your arms and embracing your perpetrators so that they can get close enough to hurt you again. Christians are instructed to have no fellowship with the unfruitful works of darkness but to expose them. Forgiveness means letting go of any ill feelings toward the perpetrators so that you can be free to think and progress in your life. Being unforgiving is self-destructive and allows your enemies to control your mind and your quality of life. Lack of forgiveness breeds bitterness resulting in severe grief, which can ultimately cause physical illness. Do not self-destruct; forgive, and true judgment will be given them at the right time. Your eyes will see it.

I was 37 years old and 7 and a half months pregnant when I met Trace by accident at the company. We made eye contact and, surprisingly, I felt secure, at ease and at peace with all his wrong doings. I had control of my life

13: Recovery

and my feelings. He looked at my maternity dress but said nothing. There was no hostility as in the past, and we both dropped our heads until I got off the elevator. I knew I had recovered because I could stand in the perpetrators' presence without ill feelings and fear.

After three years I had overcome the obstacles. But it did not happen overnight. In the beginning, I was always fearful. Then, gradually, I began to walk with confidence. I encouraged others along the way. I put on a good show until something happened to remind me of past abuse. In this instance, I was coordinating a group session, which an executive was monitoring. Toward the end of the session, he stood up and announced apologetically that he had to leave early; however, he thought that the meeting was informative. Leaving the room he softly touched my shoulder and back and said "good night" to every one in the room. Immediately, my countenance changed. I felt defiled, stripped and dominated. Past memories of the verbal and physical encounters surfaced. Paranoia gripped my thoughts as I wondered how much of my past had been discussed with this person. Needless to say I was mentally distressed and very uncomfortable in his presence from that period. Then I realized what a mess I was. Apparently, I had not healed totally from past experiences.

After a couple of months, I realized that I needed to be renewed. I needed new thoughts and new ideas. Something in me had to change. One morning, I awoke to start my day and as I entered the bathroom and began to wash my face, I looked into the mirror and a still small voice said, "wash away the old ways, old views, and the old hurts." I put down my wash rag and prayed, "Lord I need to be renewed. Give me new thoughts, new hopes, new ideas and a new attitude." When I got in the car I continued my petitions and something happened – I began to smile more, I began to see beauty in new places, and the old memories were not prevalent. I was the same person, but my attitude and outlook had changed for the better. It takes the foolish things of the world to confound the wise. How could a simple prayer be so effective? Only God knows. I do know, however that if I had harbored the old thoughts, I would have stagnated. Survival depends upon renewal and flexibility.

Joy is another component of recovery. Recent studies have shown that laughter has healed chronic diseases, it can also heal the soul. Laughter signifies confidence (faith) that the situation is under control.

A merry heart doeth good like a medicine: but a broken spirit drieth the bones.
Proverbs 17:22

Cast not away therefore your confidence, which hath great recompense of reward.

For ye have need of patience, that, after ye have done the will of God, ye might receive the promise.
Hebrews 10:35

14: Purpose In Persecution

But I say unto you, love your enemies, bless them that curse you, do good to them that hate you, and pray for them which despitefully use you and persecute you.

That ye may be the children of your Father which is in heaven: for he maketh his sun to rise on the evil and on the good, and sendeth rain on the just and on the unjust.

Matthew 5:44-45

In the quietness of my home one night the phone rang, startling my husband awake. It was 12:45 a.m. My husband picked up the receiver, listened for a moment and said, "Sharon it's for you." I couldn't imagine who would call me at 12:45 in the morning. When I picked up the phone, a troubled man's voice was on the other end. He sounded desperate, although his voice was clear and the words were firm. It was Percy, someone who had worked with me in Marketing. As members of a minority, both of us were being tormented by members of "the network" at the same time.

Percy told me that I was going to be summoned as a witness and that I would hear from his lawyer. He'd hoped that another person would testify in my stead but recently learned that the other witness died eight months before the deposition date.

He was loud and belligerent, insisting that I testify, but I wanted to put everything behind me. I responded firmly, "I will talk to you more about this later, but keep in mind that you are on the outside looking in and not me."

His voice softened while telling me that he knew I had courage to tell the truth about the situation. He did

14: Purpose In Persecution

not expect me to lie but to tell the truth. Although, I had experienced stress much longer than he, it took its toll on him immediately. Memories of the verbal abuse and the torment that both of us suffered began to resurface. I remembered his angry face as he learned about plans to eliminate us. It was horrible for him because he had believed himself one of the group. He went drinking with his colleagues and seemed to have a good business relationship with them. Then, suddenly, they turned against him. His panic, bitterness and rage grew day by day until be was unable to work. Eventually, due to stress and deep depression, he was given a medical leave. Occasionally, he called me and I would talk to him, counsel him and pray for him.

All of these memories visited me as I wondered what repercussions I would experience for witnessing on his behalf, which meant speaking against the company. I was in a no-win situation. A company lawyer called me about the deposition and my participation. She asked me what I knew of the case, and I told her of my experiences. She listened eagerly and then asked me if I knew that Percy had taped our conversations as evidence of the discrimination and harassment that took place. The lawyer shared the taped conversations, which were transcribed on paper, and I confirmed the conversations. Then she began to prepare me for the deposition by questioning me. During the course of the questioning, I noticed that I had forgotten most of the details. I also had forgotten the pain and the stress.

But as the lawyer probed, asking me more and more questions, I found myself reliving some of the most painful times in my career. My voice trembled and my eyes teared. It was like reopening an old wound that had healed. That evening, I went home and pulled out the documentation of my incidents. The more I remembered, the more the hurt came to the surface. I cried.

After this release of emotion, I was able to go to the deposition without anger toward Percy. I noticed how he had changed physically because of the stress in his life. He had lost weight and quite a bit of hair. His eyes were red and dim, and his skin hung on his bones. I could only recognize his voice. Then a still small voice, the Holy Spirit within me, reminded me of what I might have done if it were me and what I would do if I did not have religion. I remembered how I was before I received the Lord Jesus and forgiveness filled my heart.

It is easy to appreciate and enjoy the good times; it is very difficult to extract the positive out of a negative experience. But the enjoyment of weathering the negative and coming out on top is not to be described.

Here are the lessons I learned.

Looking back, the immediate persecutions have become insignificant. They are only small pieces of a puzzle which fits the big picture – the Creator's purpose in life for us and it works for our good. The pressures of life stretch us and expose the best or the worst in us. There were flaws in my character, and this trial helped me overcome them.

One of these was unforgiveness.

I have preached at churches in Michigan, at rescue missions and nursing homes telling others about Christ.

14: Purpose In Persecution

I gave food to the hungry, clothing to those who were naked and money to the needy. I volunteered as a tutor for the Detroit Public Schools and packed food for the hungry for the Gleamers Association. I had taught Sunday School, and I was a born again Christian. Everything seemed to be complete, but without charity I was nothing.

I knew that the uncontrollable anger and unforgiveness I had toward my offenders could hinder my salvation. It was almost impossible for me to forgive them. Time after time, I experienced the most extreme measures of persecutions and harassment until I learned to forgive.

Eventually, I learned to release anger and bitterness towards the perpetrators on the job and forgive them so that I could prosper. Today, it is very possible for me to work with someone who has harassed or wronged me in some way without feeling anger, strife and bitterness. I am more sensitive and compassionate to others as a result of my experiences. I am more anchored in my convictions.

Perhaps another purpose in my trial was for me to learn the strategies of harassment so that I can share them with you. While I was going through these trials, I studied the patterns and the strategies of my tormentors. At the time, I thought that I would use what I learned in a law suit against the company and that I would be monetarily compensated. However, self-gain is never the real motive for God's plan in our lives. It may be a benefit, but it cannot be the primary purpose. Saving the lives of people who are potential victims was God's plan for me and is now my sole objective. Too many people are being victimized, spending sleepless nights and miserable days at the work place. Their health is deteriorating, and their minds are being destroyed due to the unjustness discrimination, harassment and verbal abuse on the job. Life's pleasures cannot be enjoyed because of these offenses.

I have written this book to tell you that you don't have to suffer great stress because of harassment if you learn how to overcome. We are placed here on earth to work and enjoy the life given us. Do not perish for lack of knowledge. Share this information with someone who is experiencing problems on the job, or someone who is starting their careers. Share this with someone who is a victim and needs to recover from the experience.

In Gratitude

This book was divinely inspired by God. Therefore, I give all honor to God and to the unction of the Holy Ghost for this work.

About the Author

Sharon was born on July 18, 1956, in Detroit, Michigan. She is a product of the Detroit Public School System, graduating from Northwestern Senior High School. Later she obtained a Bachelor of Science Degree in General Management-Business Administration from Wayne State University.

Sharon has been married to Lester Floyd for 20 years. They have two daughters, Christina (17) and Angelice (4). Following in the path of her mother, the late Lilla Darby, who was an ordained minister of the Gospel of Jesus Christ, Sharon answered the call of God as an Evangelist. She is now the President of the Victory Tabernacle Outreach Ministries V.T.O.M. and recently started the Parent-Child Home Development Program of Detroit. It serves at-risk families with children ages 2-4, preremedial education and Christian principles at home.

Sharon has been employed for 23 years and thanks God for the many challenges that work life brings, enjoying music, exercise and family living.

As you read this book hopefully you will be touched, taught, delivered and inspired to overcome conflict in the work place.

Stand

Sharon A. Floyd

Quantity	Price Per Book	Total
	$12.95	
Shipping & Handling	$1.50	
	Total Amount Enclosed	

❏ Cash ❏ Check ❏ Money Order

Make checks and money orders payable to:
Sharon Floyd

Mail To:
Victory Tabernacle Outreach Ministries
P.O. Box 38746
Detroit, Michigan 48238-9998
SHIP TO:

_____

_____

_____